Predestined
IN MY
Purpose

Mary A. Newman Baldwin, PhD

WESTBOW
PRESS®
A DIVISION OF THOMAS NELSON
& ZONDERVAN

WestBow Press books may be ordered through booksellers or by contacting:

WestBow Press
A Division of Thomas Nelson & Zondervan
1663 Liberty Drive
Bloomington, IN 47403
www.westbowpress.com
844-714-3454

Scripture taken from the King James Version of the Bible.

ISBN: 978-1-6642-0416-4 (sc)
ISBN: 978-1-6642-0418-8 (hc)
ISBN: 978-1-6642-0417-1 (e)

Library of Congress Control Number: 2020916779

Print information available on the last page.

WestBow Press rev. date: 11/30/2020

For I know the thoughts that I think toward you, saith the Lord, thoughts of peace, and not of evil to bring you to an expected end.

Jeremiah 29:11 KJV

Contents

What Is Your Worth?

One of the most important questions a person has ever asked me was "What is your worth?" At the time, I did not understand the question. I later learned the person was asking me what value I placed on myself. What was the outcome I expected for myself in any given situation? Am I better than the things I allowed to occur in my life? Am I better than the things that happened to me that I had no control over? Am I better than the hand that life has dealt me? My answer was, "Yes, I am." We cannot govern what other people do or say to us or the hand that life has dealt us, but we can control how we react to it.

Worth, as defined by *Merriam-Webster's Dictionary,* means to have monetary or material value. I was being asked what my self-worth was. What was the value I placed upon myself? What was my value measurement according to my qualities or self-esteem that governed me? Was I better than the sexual abuse I encountered as a child? Was I better than allowing someone to cheat on me, lie to me, or even lie on me? Was I better than the lies I was expected to believe? Was I better than the job I settled for? More importantly, was I better than that broken woman who faced me every morning when I looked in the mirror? That broken woman who had endured so many traumatic experiences during her lifetime that she felt as if her life was set up to fail, and every bad thing that she encountered, she deserved.

For so long, we have allowed society to tell us what things make us valuable. The way we dress, look, our weight, height, beauty, social status, success, the type of car we drive, type of house or community we live in, or what brand of clothes we wear. These are insignificant things that add no more value to us than if we were without them. No, none of these things can ever define a person's worth. Not mine, not yours, not anyone on earth. There are people living on the streets whose worth is far greater than yours or mine. You will never see it judging by their appearances. How misleading has society become? And we accept it.

What adds value to us is our character, integrity, morals, and life experiences. Life does not care about any of society's attributes. It does not discriminate based on any of society's "values." And guess what—life happens to us all. We are all shaped by our life experiences, some for the good, and some for the better. But all life experiences shape us into who we are to become and help us get where we need to be. What life *does* care about is how we overcome these experiences and what we do with the experiences we have overcome.

No matter what traumas we have faced, we have the power within us to overcome any of life's situations. The power within each of us is stronger than anything life can throw our way.

I had a discussion about the hereditary aspect of people who excessively drink alcohol, use drugs, or are promiscuous. My friend stated that the trait has to come from somewhere. We then go back and look at the actions displayed by members of the same family and make the conclusion that it must be hereditary. We even call them *generational curses.* When something is hereditary, we have no control over it, i.e., the natural color of our eyes, hair, complexion, or height. However, we can control all other external forces, such as alcoholism, drugs, or overeating. These are conscious choices that we make. For every issue that makes people feel they have to succumb to life's challenges, there have been multiple people who faced the same issues and successfully overcame them.

When we make such statements, we do not realize we are attempting to justify our shortcomings. In doing so, we take away the need to be responsible and accountable for our actions. Everyone has their own individual choices to make concerning how they want to live. But we must learn to conquer these external forces and not allow them to subdue us.

We have heard alcoholism referred to in the medical terminology as a disease, taking away the drinker's need to be accountable and responsible, saying he or she cannot help drinking—it's hereditary—and citing that his or her mother or father was an alcoholic. But when he or she has an accident and kills somebody, we want to hold them accountable for drinking and driving. People make the conscious choice to drink excessively, even though it has been proven to cause cirrhosis of the liver. People make the choice to use drugs, knowing the outcome of their use. We are living in a time when we need to take back control over our own lives. If no one else does, we need to hold ourselves responsible and accountable for our actions and the choices we make, good or bad.

We live in a society of people who are hurting, a society of people who have not yet found the strength to say that my circumstances, disappointments, feelings of rejection (or whatever has shaped who you are) will not keep me from obtaining my destiny, as opposed to giving in because they cannot see clearly how the moment will end. A society of people who would rather bury the pain caused by their traumatic life experiences in a bottle of alcohol, drugs, or illicit sex, than to muster up the strength and courage to be vulnerable and say, "I have a problem. I need to get help to overcome it. I will not be defeated."

I do not claim to have the answers. Although I do believe that every encounter we have leads us one step closer to our greater cause or purpose. Wherever we find ourselves at this particular moment in time is exactly where we are supposed to be, and we are doing exactly what we are supposed to be doing. This very life experience is preparing us for our greater purpose. Purpose is the one thing every creation on earth has. All of our purposes were designed for the greater good of all humanity. Whether we have a positive or negative impact on society is up to us. Whether good or bad, it will all work together for our benefit.

For years, we all have been conditioned to look and act as if everything is okay; to act as if we have no worries or flaws; to be a perfect example of how people should look and act. In actuality, most of us either are victims or have been victims in the past. Some people are able to overcome their traumatic life experiences, while others sometimes become the predators, succumbing to the very thing they can't seem to overcome. They continue the pattern from prior generations simply because they do not know how to process the information from their own traumatic life experiences.

Learning to recognize and confront these issues is the only way a person can begin the healing process. (We will discuss in further detail.) Talking about the experiences with a confidant, psychiatrist, life coach, or spiritual counselor is a very good start on the road to healing. Remember, whatever demons you face, your monster will never be what the public sees. Monsters do not come out when the light is shining. They live in darkness, so as not to be detected.

Today we hear more and more stories of sexual abuse being courageously told by survivors who suffered abuse at the hands of someone they knew, loved, and trusted. Some of these abusers were from prestigious backgrounds. Many victims as well as their abusers struggle with mental issues, rejection, and other forms of abuse.

Though we cannot ignore the fact that among real reports of abuse, there are also fabricated stories told by those who seek attention, money, or just to tear down someone's reputation and character. Let me interject here. When it comes to such claims, we should not put anything past anyone. By the same token, let's make sure that we are telling the truth when we make such claims. Once these accusatory words are spoken, they can never be taken back or retracted. Even if you confess it was all a lie, that stigma is forever embedded in the minds of the individuals as well as the public.

Secondly, when false claims of any type are made, those claims can diminish the power of claims that are valid. The falsehood makes it hard for people who are victims of such an ordeal to not only speak out but get the justice they deserve. Being a victim of sexual abuse is never an easy truth to face. A person has to relive those horrific moments every time they tell their story and be judged from the moment they open their mouths. Everyone reacts to traumatic experiences in different ways. But believe me, *everyone* reacts.

It is said that abused people grow up and become abusers. Could this be because they have not learned to process what has happened to them in their earlier lives? Maybe they were too afraid to tell someone what was happening to them. Maybe they enjoyed the feeling it gave them and were somehow ashamed. Maybe they thought it was how love was supposed to feel. Maybe they blamed themselves. Whatever the reason, you need someone to help you process it. You need to know it was not your fault. You did not deserve what happened to you. You need to break the cycle of abuse in your own life, the abuse from your abuser as well as your self-inflicted abuse.

Thirdly you need to learn how to forgive the person who has violated you. If at all possible, go to them. Let them know how their violation of you made you feel. Let them know the effect it had on you. But more importantly, let them know that you will not let it define who you are or who you will become. If the person is no longer living, it may help to visit the gravesite to release the anger. Write a letter, addressing it to the perpetrator, and then burn it up, tear it up, or flush it down the toilet. Any way you can release your anger and guilt is what you need to do.

There is nothing wrong with screaming, crying, or shouting to get the anger out of your system. Some people use punching bags, break things, or work out. As long as you are not hurting others. You need to release as much of the negative energy as possible.

If you are the perpetrator, the worst thing you can do to your victim is deny that you have ever violated or harmed them in any way. You owe it to yourself and the victim to take responsibility for your actions. You need to ask them for their forgiveness and try to make amends. Denying the role you played in their traumatic experience only adds insult to injury. Don't play the blame game. What happened to you (the perpetrator) as a child should not be your reason for inflicting the same type of pain on the next person. If so, maybe you need to go to your abuser and get the same type of release.

We need to understand that people are not the way they are simply because that is how they want to be. They have been conditioned to display certain behaviors due to their life's experiences, in which some feel they have no other alternative. Many of these life experiences we had no control over, yet we have allowed them to maintain control over us. We have allowed them to dictate who we are and what we can and cannot do. It is time we take back our own lives. It is time we realize that our life experiences are all part of a greater plan.

God knew that the day would come when there would be an outpouring of people who suffered from the same things you encountered. God knew he would cause you to use your life experiences to help those people through their trials.

Over the centuries, we have become a blameless society. No longer do we accept responsibility for our own actions, but look to place the blame elsewhere. The truth is we make the choice to do the things we do.

So, what do we do with all this negative energy floating around in the universe? How do we replace the negative with the good? How do we find the right energy to emit to the universe? How do we cope with our traumatic life experiences? How do we as a society begin the healing process?

If you have ever heard the phrase, "When life gives you lemons, you make lemonade," that is exactly what you do.

The first thing that any good lemonade maker knows is that you must prepare to make the lemonade. In preparing, you need the following items: a lemon, container, water, sugar, and an agitator or something to stir the contents. All of these items are equally important if you are going to make good lemonade.

The Lemons

"When life gives you lemons, you make lemonade"

There are multiple uses for lemons. The lemons equate to one's life experiences. Your life experiences set the foundation for what's to come in your future. No two lemons are exactly the same, and neither are your experiences.

A single lemon alone can leave a sour taste in your mouth. The more lemons you add to the lemonade, the stronger the sour taste will become. As with your life experiences, the more negative experiences you encounter, the more sour or bitter an individual may become. As long as you have breath in your body, you will encounter lemons in some measure.

Over time, encountering life's traumatic experiences can cause the human body to produce acidic juices that can erode a person's very core. Lemons also contain many seeds, which all have the potential to produce other lemons when planted and cultivated. The fact that lemons are produced by thorny trees makes hand-picking them more difficult. There is a good chance that a person will get stuck at least once by the thorns. As with life experiences, some lessons are harder than others. Each experience leaves seeds that have the potential to either be positive or negative, thereby producing fruits after its own kind. Some sticks are worse than others, and some sticks may go deeper into the skin than others.

8

Proper medical attention to the wounds can prevent further medical issues such as infections. Some infections can be cured with over-the-counter medication, while others are cured with prescription medication; still others may require hospitalization or even surgery. In the most extreme cases, if not treated, some infections can lead to death.

As in life, choosing which lemon to use has little to do with us or our decisions but more to do with God's perfect plan for our lives. God, in His infinite wisdom, has already written our lives from beginning to end, even before we were formed in our mother's womb. From the time of birth, we began our preparation in life to our destined purpose. The family we were born into was already hand-chosen to help prepare us for our purpose. No matter what our experience (good or bad) with our family, we are in preparation mode for our destiny to fulfill our purpose.

Before you were born, the city and state in which you live, the number of siblings in your family, your name, and date of birth had already been chosen and play a very important role in what's to come in your future. The things we endure during this stage in life help us to recognize our strengths, weaknesses, gifts, and passions. This conditioning and grooming help develop our uniqueness or characteristics for who or what we will grow up to become.

The morals and values instilled in us as children, our experiences, challenges, and lessons learned during this time, all prepare us for the next stage in our lives. In a child's early years, if asked what he or she wants to be when he or she grows up, the most common answers are doctors, teachers, or firemen. Why? Because these are the professions that children meet more than any others. Each occupation is geared toward the betterment of others. Their experiences with these sectors help prepare them for these professions.

As young children, we are endowed with a sense of helping others in need. Children are not born with a selfish nature;

selfishness is a learned behavior, just like hate. We were all created with an assignment to love others and a purpose for the betterment of the world. Yes, even as children, we are subconsciously wired to want to help others. No child who has been raised in a toxic environment says he or she wants to be a rapist, molester, abuser, or alcoholic. Yet so many have these in their testimony.

During this stage in our lives, we are dealing with pressures placed on us by our families, friends, and society as a whole. Not being able to openly discuss many of life's experiences with others only further causes us to isolate ourselves. Not having a safe outlet when needed often causes us to explode outwardly. Isolation in some instances can be good because it gives individuals an opportunity to examine themselves to see how a particular experience is to be used as knowledge for their purpose.

Parents take the time to share many of their life experiences with their children, in hopes that it will keep them from making the same mistakes they made. When it is you living the experience, you are unable to see the magnitude of the lesson from a level plane. It is not until you are able to see the experience from a higher perspective that you realize how the experiences have prepared you for your purpose. Life lessons were meant to be taught, and we were meant to learn from them. The lessons we learned were meant to be used to help the next person who is dealing with similar experiences.

We cannot and should not try to take responsibility for another person. In doing so, we steal away their life lessons, their appointments to grow, and their chances at securing their own freedom.

The Container

Choosing the right container will determine the amount of lemonade that can be made at any one time. The size of your container will determine the amount of experiences you will be able to handle. Depending on the assignment, some people require multiple life experiences, while others require only minimal experiences. Nevertheless, it all equals out.

The container represents you, the person. Containers come in all shapes and sizes. The shape does not matter as much as its size.

Some containers were made to hold small amounts of substances, while others were meant to hold larger amounts. Each size is chosen based on the amount needed for a specific purpose. As with each individual person, our life experiences and the amounts of experiences we can hold are predicated upon the number of people we are purposed to reach. Some people may be assigned five, and others five thousand. But whether five or five thousand, each purpose is just as important as the next.

During this phase, we will evaluate those life experiences (whether bad or good) to decide which to keep and which to reject. We will evaluate the lessons we have learned from these experiences and whether or not they have enhanced our lives or taken away from our lives. This is where we take a stand and decide whether or not we will continue in the experience, come what may, or walk away from it altogether.

After we have made our decision, confirmation is sure to come by way of a conversation with someone, dreams, visions, a television show or video on the topic that confirms our decision, or simply a gut feeling letting you know you have made the right decision.

All of life's challenges and lessons prepare us for our destiny, and we must be able to hold the information that's given to us. This is the defining moment that prompts us to realize what we were created to be. Not all lessons and challenges in life are pleasant.

Things we plant are usually placed in the ground and covered up with dirt. In the physical sense, we call this a burial. In other words, we must die to ourselves. We must surrender our own wants and desires and aim for the higher calling. Remember, God's thoughts and plans for our lives are far greater than anything we can ever hope, dream, or imagine for ourselves. That said, we can no longer think *me* but must think *us*. How will the information from my experiences help others overcome their similar situations?

This is the stage when we begin to walk into what or who we were created to be. We now have some sense of direction. We know the what, when, where, why, and how of the matter. This is also the stage when God begins to cultivate us. During cultivation, as we grow, God begins to cut away at the grass growing around us, to keep it from smothering us out. He continuously tills the soil around us to ensure it is fit for our growth.

Cultivation is the removal of anything or any person from our lives that hinders our growth or gets us off course, such as family members, longtime friends, colleagues, jobs, houses, cars, or social status. Anything that interferes with us being able to do God's will. It can be allowing us to lose everything we hold dear, to move us to a place where we can hear God's voice and His voice only.

As we begin to grow, cultivation takes place in each phase of our lives, introducing us to people with whom we will need to connect to retrieve information and discarding that relationship once it no longer serves a purpose in our future. We have to decipher which relationships we need to keep and which we need to terminate.

It is important that as we go through life, we remember that relationships are designed to either teach us a lesson or for us to teach someone else a lesson, but not meant to lie dormant. If a relationship is dormant or becomes dormant, it may no longer serve a purpose in your life. Do not be afraid to let go and walk away.

The Water

Water is a liquid that descends from the clouds as rain; forms streams, lakes, and seas; and is essential to all life. All lifeforms dissolve water and feed off its nutrients, which are needed for growth. Without water, life as we know it would exist no more. Your life experiences are those trials and encounters that help shape you into the person you need to become to reach your destiny and fulfill your purpose.

As with the trials one faces during his or her life, without these experiences, there would be no growth, individually or otherwise. All the good and bad experiences life has thrown our way are needed to promote a healthy individual capable of being a productive citizen.

Water in and of itself is shapeless, yet when placed in a container, water takes the shape of the container. Think about this: as water flows along the stream or river, it changes its shape to fit the space available. When water is placed in a glass, it takes the shape of the glass. When water is poured onto a plate or into a bowl, the amount of water remains the same, but its shape changes.

How should we look at life experiences? All of our experiences, whether good or bad, are the right conditions to ensure growth. During these experiences, you will connect with the right people, who will assist you with information, tools, and equipment needed for your purpose. These are people who have been assigned to help you during your growth stage.

During this stage, you will experience events that will help you soar to the next level. You may also face some adversity and challenges that may shake your very core. Adversity and difficult challenges are not designed to destroy you but strengthen you. Like a good farmer prunes away at a plant to keep it growing healthy, adversity prunes away the dead things in your life that can hinder your growth. Dead things are the people and situations that no longer serve a purpose in your life. After the pruning, the plant may look odd, but once the plant has matured, it becomes the most beautiful creation.

Every person we encounter in our lives serves a purpose. That purpose has either a positive or negative effect. It is up to each of us to choose what we will do with the information that has been deposited in us. We have to learn the lesson that was taught and get ready to move to the next chapter of our story. Even when we experience setbacks, we are to remember that setbacks are like yield signs that let us know we are not ready to proceed to the next chapter of our lives. Setbacks can be God's way of keeping us safe from harm or letting us know that there are more lessons to learn. The purpose of setbacks is to strengthen, help, and give us time to grow into what we were created to be at that particular moment.

Growth occurs when you can look at all of life's worst experiences and see the good. You can see that the things you thought were meant to take you out were actually blessings in disguise. Yes! There is an old adage, "There is a blessing in the storm." Often blessings are disguised as horrific events meant to turn your world upside down, to stop you from reaching your destiny and achieving your purpose. In hindsight, even the worst of these experiences can be a cultivating ground for you to start over and rebuild on a sturdier foundation. No matter how many times you fall or get knocked down, make the choice to get back up.

No matter what anyone tells you, you must get back up. Your purpose is greater than anyone's opinion of you and even greater than your own opinion of yourself. Our thoughts of ourselves outweigh the thoughts of others. We are more critical of ourselves than anyone else, and we find it hard to forgive ourselves if we fail. The fear of failure is always paralyzing us and our dreams. It is our fear that keeps us from becoming who or what we were created to be. We can be so cautious of failing that fear sets in and keeps us from moving toward our goals.

There is no such thing as being predestined to fail. We were predestined to be victorious before the foundation of the world. We are predestined to be winners. We are equipped with everything we need to overcome any obstacle that stands in our way. The tools we possess lay dormant inside of us, waiting to be unleashed.

Growth is not always comfortable. As we grow, we encounter many adversities and challenges, often more difficult than the last one. But it is these adversities and challenges that strengthen our roots. When God begins to grow us, often we do not realize what is taking place until after the test or trial. We feel uncomfortable or out of place. For some, it may seem as though your whole world has been turned upside down. Relax, it is only God's way of making sure He has your complete and undivided attention. We can rest assured that every aspect of what we have encountered in life will be utilized. Not one ounce of it will be lost, whether good or bad.

During our stages of growth, sometimes the tests become so powerful and overwhelming that we want to throw in the towel. We cannot understand why God is allowing these things to come upon us. We question why. To the naked eyes of men, God is punishing us. But to God, He is preparing us to reach our destiny to fulfill our purpose.

This is the moment when our seeds give birth. The seeds we have planted in God's will begin to grow, and our roots begin to spread. The moment we decide to surrender ourselves is the exact moment our growth begins. The moment we surrender to God's perfect will for our lives, God will move heaven and earth to ensure our growth. Growth is the outcome of us successfully completing life's most challenging experiences. In every stage of life, there is room for growth.

Cultivating and pruning are still a major part of the growth process, as well as the cutting away of people and things no longer needed. We receive nourishment that helps us grow until we reach our final stage. The more we water a plant, the bigger the plant grows.

Everything we have experienced in our lives prepares us to live the purpose for which we were created. The length of time it takes to reach our destiny depends on each individual person, the lessons needed to be learned, and the amount of time it takes to teach them. But do not worry—where you are right now, at this very moment, is exactly where God planned for you to be.

The closer we get to realizing our purpose, the stronger that resistance becomes. When you are faced with multiple crucial moments, just know that you are getting closer to your purpose. Keep telling yourself you must remain focused on the finish line, accomplishing your purpose. The resistance is only to keep us from realizing that purpose. In every ill-fated experience we go through, there is a hidden blessing inside that will lead us to our purpose.

One morning as I was walking up a steep hill, I was reminded that life is just like walking up a steep hill. The closer you get to the top, the harder it is to climb. But if you can just stay focused on getting to the top of the hill, you are going to make it. You cannot afford to take your eyes off the goal (reaching the top of the hill). Every now and then, you may encounter a pothole in the road. There may be an obstruction in your path. You may not be able to see around the corner. You may even experience a strong current of wind pushing you back and preventing you from continuing to climb the hill. These are only temporary distractions. You must keep telling yourself that you must reach the top of the hill.

Sometimes, you may have to take smaller steps, setting smaller goals within the realm of the larger goal. Focus on the enjoyment you are going to have when you reach the top of the hill. Focus on the satisfaction you will receive. We are all faced with the ultimate test, one that can make or break us. We have to be watered and cultivated over and over until we reach maturity. We endure test after test, trial after trial, heartache after heartache, disappointment after disappointment, and yet, the process is repeated with each of these.

No matter how much good we do, we are still met with opposition. We must withstand the resistance in order to reach our destiny. Resistance is the first step to change. As with climbing that steep hill, the wind is in front of you, pushing you back, trying to keep you from reaching your purpose, but once you reach the top of the hill, on the other side is all downhill, and the force of the wind is behind you, pushing you forward.

I know it is hard to maintain a positive outlook on life and circumstances when all we see is the negativity. It seems impossible to maintain one's faith when trials become too powerful and overwhelming. Very few people have mastered dealing with the unknown, so many people give up during this stage in life.

In order to properly grow in the growth season of our lives, we need to make sure that we do not listen to the opinions of others. We must maintain a positive attitude and get rid of our fears. We must not give in to doubt, as it will stunt our growth and keep us from flourishing into the productive individuals we were created to be.

The Sugar

Sugar is an important source of dietary carbohydrate and a sweetener and preservative of other foods. The more sugar you add to foods, the sweeter it will taste. The sweetness of the lemonade is determined by the person preparing it. As with making lemonade, the growth process depends on the person.

This is the stage of manifestation; the time when we decide whether or not we will allow our life's traumatic experiences to make us bitter or make us better. If we choose bitterness, we have succumbed to defeat. We are denying the very thing for which we were created, a greater purpose. The place where our preparation, demanding work, growth, and faith throughout our trials have paid off. By choosing to become better, we are able to serve others and watch the joy on their faces. It is the satisfaction that what you have spent time preparing the lemonade for is able to quench the thirst (need) of others.

It is the moment when our faith and belief in ourselves produces much fruit for the benefit of others. In a sense, it is the law of reaping and sowing. We walk into a wealthy place, because the more we give (pour out), the more we are compensated. It is a place where there is no lack. The fruits of our labor are now being used to benefit others. It is a chance to see our fruits in action, being passed from one person to the next and generations to come.

During this season, we are able to look back over our lives and see just how all our life's experiences fit perfectly together to groom us for this moment. It is here that we see the value of those traumatic experiences and the process it took to get us to this stage in life. Yes, everything we have learned from our past has prepared us for this exact moment. Many people say, "I see why I had to go through the things I went through." One thing is very certain: whether it is our doing or part of the plan of God, it will *all* work for our good.

I have heard many people compare purpose to an onion. "It must be peeled back one layer at a time." Now I understand what they meant. It unfolds everything in our lives that has prepared us to live the purpose we were created to fulfill. The biggest challenge we all face is knowing what purpose is and finding the courage to follow it. Once we have accomplished these things, we must learn how to live in our purpose in the face of adversity.

Each path to recognizing one's purpose is different. No two are the same. Although they may have many similarities, they are still different. We can have the same title but each have a different function or purpose. How we deal with life experiences is different for each person. There is no right or wrong way to deal with life's experiences, but I will say, the sooner you learn the lesson, the sooner you are able to move on to your life's next experience.

Life is a symphony in which we all exist to create in its entirety. We each have our own unique note that we are destined to play. Each note was destined before we were formed in our mother's womb and can only be played by that individual. This reminds me of one of my favorite songs by Yolanda Adams. It is a beautiful ballad that reminds us God is in complete and total control of our lives. The song simply says, "I am the composer of the melody of life. So, take upon my yoke and learn of me, I'll be your guiding light. I am the director, be part of my symphony." Whether or not a person accepts this request is his or her personal decision that can only be made by him or her. However, your acceptance has already been prepared, and the place has already been designated. It's up to you to walk forward.

Life is all about experiencing life, not just merely existing in it. What are you going to do with these experiences? Yes, they are for you in that moment but also preparing you to reach others in the future. You cannot tell a person how to overcome a situation that you neither experienced nor overcame.

As with any crop, we should all want to produce good fruit. Fruit produces seeds in others that will change their hearts, their lives, and their beliefs.

Our life's purpose is all about becoming the person we were born to be in this life. It is the guiding system that provides us with direction. Once we realize we are on the right path, we will find passion, confidence, and strength to go after those dreams. Purpose gives us a reason to live. If we search deep within our hearts and are honest with ourselves, our hearts will let us know what our purpose is. The heart does not lie.

For the world to change, we the people have to change. We have to change our beliefs as well as ourselves. If we change our beliefs, we can change our behaviors, habits, and outcomes. We have to change the way we look at the world, our situations, and others. Changing the world can happen one person at a time.

The Agitator

Once all the ingredients have been placed in the container, you will need something to stir these ingredients, mixing them together so they can fully dissolve. It is important that these ingredients are allowed the opportunity to dissolve completely; otherwise, they will leave a gritty, unpleasant taste in your mouth.

To complete this phase of making the lemonade, you will need a utensil long enough to reach the bottom of the container, to stir the ingredients. This utensil acts as an agitator. An agitator is a tool used for stirring liquid. When washing clothes, it is the part of a washing machine that moves the water and clothes from side to side so that the water, laundry detergent, bleach, and fabric softener are dissolved throughout the water. The more clothes in the washer, the harder it will be for the agitator to move and adequately clean the clothes.

The length of the utensil used is determined by the depth of the container. The more ingredients you put in the container, the more difficult it is to stir the ingredients and the longer time it will take for the ingredients to dissolve.

As with our life experiences, the more dead weight, unresolved issues, people, and unproductive things surrounding us, the harder it is for us to grow properly. Too many dead leaves on a plant will eventually cause the entire plant to wither away and die.

When a person makes lemonade, the ingredients need to be

stirred until they are completely dissolved. Once these ingredients dissolve, the lemonade is ready to be served to quench the thirst of others. Even if the lemonade is agitated, it will not lose its form. None of its ingredients will separate. No matter how many times you stir or shake it up, it remains unbothered. In life, the more unforgiveness and bitterness we house inside of us, the less likely we will be able to properly heal. Even the slightest bump can cause bleeding.

I liken the agitator to being spiritually delivered from something. If you are truly delivered and set free from something, no matter what comes your way or how life beats you down, you have no desire to return to it.

As with life's experiences, once we have learned the lessons, we will be able to serve others. In serving others, we will be able to assist them with their problems from the information we have gathered from life's lessons. Being able to share those experiences with others so they will not fall into the same traps is what we should all strive for.

Recognizing Your Purpose

Every person, place, and thing on earth was created with a purpose. Purpose is the reason why something or someone is created. It is the aim or intention of something. There are some people whose purpose is to encourage and aid others in achieving their goals, while others' purpose is to be the achiever. Our greatest challenges likely will serve as the preparation to help us live and share our greater purpose.

Every circumstance you have faced in your past has prepared you for this moment. Your purpose, your desire to make a difference in the world and in the lives of others. More often than not, purpose is born out of some of our most difficult challenges and deepest pains. Those experiences have prepared us for the greatest assignment of our lives.

"Life is all about learning lessons." Each of us must learn the lessons being taught and move on to our next level. It is these lessons that will lay the foundation for the purpose we are to fulfill. I promise you not one of these life experiences will be wasted. No, not one tittle. Everything we have been through, everything we have learned up to this point is exactly what will be needed to carry us through the remainder of our time here on earth. "You only meet you in life," and every person or experience we encounter is a mirror of our own inner beliefs.

"Life is what we make it." Our success in life is based on

how well we deal with those unfavorable circumstances. Will we buckle under pressure or stand tall in the face of adversity? The graver the situations we face, the greater the purpose. The greater our purpose, the greater our destiny. Everyone's purpose is just as important as the next. We may be called to fulfill the same purpose but assigned different functions within that purpose. The will, the purpose, and the destiny, although different, will eventually lead us to the same outcome.

The desire of every person who has ever lived was and is to be able to recognize and work in their purpose. There is something satisfying about accomplishing the tasks we were placed on earth to do. It is in our purpose that we find a sense of fulfillment that so many people spend a lifetime searching for. Many of us, at a very young age, have had an inner instinct, a sense that says *my contribution to the world is bigger than what I am doing now or who I am now.*

All growth has distinct phases or stages to go through. Think about it. There are growth stages in plant life, manufactured goods, diseases, education, and humans (from infancy to adulthood). Each of these phases or stages is filled with various life experiences that we will need to learn in order to reach our destiny and fulfill our purpose. Each experience leads us to a different place. With each of these experiences, we progress one step closer to our purpose.

Your purpose, both personally and universally, determines your soul path, your spiritual work, and the experiences you will have in life. In order to recognize your purpose, you will need a clear path to see it. This means you will need to remove all the negative energy from your experience, forgive, and let go. Then and only then will you be able to see the greater good of the experience and how you will be able to use it to benefit others.

When it comes to recognizing your purpose, your ministry is your *why,* and your why is your purpose. A person's ministry is often that which has brought us the most pain. It is the one thing that seems as though it will wipe us off the face of this earth. Contrary to widespread belief, ministry is not isolated to the church, but it all works together to edify and build up the church and kingdom of God. In the same instance, our purpose is not just deemed for the church but for the world at large.

I have often been met with opposition when I make this statement, but there are people strategically planted in different parts of this world who have a desire to make a difference or positive impact in that area. If we all were destined to only affect the church, the world would be in a worse condition than it is in today.

Recognizing what your purpose is can be one of the most challenging tasks you will face. *Now that I have this experience, what do I do with it?* We look for confirmation or a sense of assurance that tells us we made the right decision and are on the right path. Confirmation of purpose can come through prayer, conversations, convictions, signs, television shows, books, magazines, or gut feelings we may have.

Often our worst experiences or the thing that causes us the most pain is where our purpose lies. That thing that we are most passionate about is where we realize our purpose. Wherein our purpose lies, there is a sense of making life better for the next person.

It is possible to achieve one's purpose without achieving one's destiny, but it is impossible to achieve one's destiny without purpose. Achieving your personal goals is not the same as achieving your destiny. It is only when we recognize our purpose and achieve our destiny that we will find complete satisfaction.

PRAYER

Father,
I come to you repenting of all sins; whether knowing
or unknowing, and ask your forgiveness.
I thank you for allowing me to experience the
experiences I have encountered.
I know there is a greater purpose than myself.
Father, help me to recognize my purpose so that I may
reach those assigned to me through my testimonies.
It is well with my soul.
I let go and release it all to you.
In Jesus's name I pray.
Amen

What Now?

Most people will tell you to pray. Although I am a faithful advocate of prayer, praying alone is not the answer. You will need help in order to face the issues, deal with them, and overcome them. No one can walk this journey alone. There are people assigned to you and strategically placed to aid you in your walk. Having someone to talk to who has been through the same issues you are facing is a start. They are more likely to be empathetic to how you are feeling. For those who are not afraid to speak about what they have overcome, it can be a helpful sign to the person now dealing with the issue that all is not lost.

Don't allow anyone to make you stop talking about your life experiences. Talking is therapeutic. Talking about what you have been through allows you to release the hurt and pain. It also allows you to see yourself and the role that you play. In talking, you are able to see details you may have previously missed. If you step away from the situation and revisit it later, you may be able to see the role that you played more clearly. The most important thing is it allows you to rationalize what your next step should be.

Every time I see previews of shows dealing with zombies, it reminds me of the state of the world. We are a nation of walking wounded individuals who are too fearful or prideful to ask for help; too fearful to be vulnerable at the hands of a counselor, psychiatrist, elder, or anyone who can give us sound counsel.

We self-diagnose our symptoms and self-medicate accordingly. Whether it be illicit sex, religion, alcohol, or drugs, we are losing the battle. We are too ashamed to ask for help, for fear of being judged or someone using our confession against us.

Western culture has been referred to as the "microwave culture." We are so busy with our everyday lives, we do not take the time to stop and smell the roses, let alone have time to deal with our own issues or listen to someone else's issues.

We all need to practice taking the time to listen, as people are crying out for help. We need to recognize or discern what is wrong, even if a person does not speak. We are the walking wounded, a society of wounded individuals who have mastered masking the hurt, pain, insecurities, etc., unable to be vulnerable to anything or anyone.

We resent anything and anybody that has ever caused us harm, not realizing that resentment is anger that has been lodged and rooted deep within the body. After a while, that resentment may cause physical illness such as ulcers, tumors, and cancers.

For this reason, it is imperative that we learn how to deal with our issues. The seeds of resentment, anger, bitterness, or other negative emotions produce more seeds. These seeds, over time, begin to grow and blossom into plants with roots.

There are many people who choose not to deal with their issues. Most are ashamed, embarrassed, or just do not want to or know how to deal with their issues at that particular time. Unaddressed issues, whether mental or spiritual, can take on physical attributes such as weight gain, weight loss, skin discoloration, premature aging, and as mentioned before, illnesses within the body.

We must get to the place where we know it takes a strong person to ask forgiveness for the things he or she has done. In asking for forgiveness, we are releasing all the negative energy that comes from within.

PRAYER

Father,
I come to you repenting of all sins, whether knowing
or unknowing, and ask your forgiveness.
I thank you for allowing me this experience with (you
may insert name of the person, place or thing).
I know that you have greater purpose than myself or them
(you may insert name of the person, place or thing).
Allow us to see you and your purpose for each of us
through this experience and realize that experience
was one we all needed to learn and grow from.
Release all the negative energies from both of us so that
we may walk in a newness of mind and forgiveness.
Father, I release into your hands all the negativity associated with my
experience with (you may insert name of the person, place or thing).
I release (you may insert name of the person, place or
thing) to you with the understanding that they did what
they thought they had to do at that particular time.
I hold no bitterness, regrets, or resentment.
It is well with my soul.
I let go and release it all to you.
In Jesus's name I pray.
Amen

Forgive Yourself

Forgiving yourself is one of the hardest things you will ever have to do. It forces you to remember the very thing most people have tried to forget. Forgiving yourself forces you to remember everything that has been done to you by the people who did it. It forces you to face your weaknesses and vulnerability. Forgiveness forces you to deal with emotions that you do not want to remember—the guilt, shame, hurt, feelings of being the fool that come from being taken advantage of or being rejected.

Before you are able to forgive anyone else, you must first forgive yourself. If you cannot forgive yourself, you will not have the capacity to forgive others. I believe it is vitally important to forgive yourself for the negative things that happened to you, even though you had no control over the situation. You cannot control what others have done to you, but you can control how you react to what they have done. It is not until you are able to forgive yourself that you will see how all of these life experiences are part of a much bigger picture and how you can use those experiences to strengthen others.

Just like the pitcher of lemonade, if the container is full, no more lemonade can go inside. It is not until the substance in the pitcher has been poured out that it can be replenished. Likewise, unforgiveness consumes your entire being. It consumes the inside as well as the outside of your body. No positive energy can go in or be released. The only way to replace the negativity with positivity is to release the negative energy. Emotions are a conscious mental reaction or strong feelings toward a specific object that causes physiological and behavioral changes in our bodies, while our feelings are our thoughts in action.

Forgiving ourselves is an act of freedom. You are freeing yourself from all the negativity associated with that experience. Forgiveness is more beneficial to you than the person who has wronged you. More often than not, the person for whom you hold unforgiveness has moved on with life, and you remain stuck in the past. Now you need to move forward into your future as well. Release yourself. Stop holding yourself hostage to a past that has no future for you.

Forgiveness is the most powerful weapon you possess. Learn to walk in forgiveness on a daily basis, expecting nothing from others but who they truly are, expecting no less from yourself than who you truly are.

Learning to forgive yourself produces self-love, the most important gift we can give ourselves. Whitney Houston said it best with her song which said, "Learning to love yourself; it is the greatest love of all." But how do you forgive yourself? I have developed the following exercise to help in self-forgiveness. You may perform the exercise as many times as needed.

EXERCISE

Light a white candle. Then begin to pray and denounce all the negative energy from your past experiences and disappointments.

Pray and release all your fears and guilt associated with such disappointments. These could be feelings of inadequacy, rejection, failed business ventures, family, divorce, loss of close friends or family members.

Pray and release yourself from the blame you took on for not accomplishing what you feel you should have accomplished by now. You are exactly where you were predestined to be at this exact moment. Learn to accept the fact that it happened, it was all a part of a much bigger plan that has already been prepared, and you can release yourself from the things you had no control over.

PRAYER

Father,
I come to you repenting of all sins, whether knowing
or unknowing, and ask your forgiveness.
I thank you for allowing me the opportunity
to learn from my life experiences.
I know that you have greater purpose than myself.
I pray and release myself from all the fear, guilt, shame,
and blame I placed on me from my life experiences.
I am exactly where I have been predestined to
be at this specific time in my life.
I am on schedule to reach my destiny.
I love and accept me, all of me (the good and the bad),
knowing that in you I am complete and made whole.
I hold no blame against anyone or anything involved,
for only I can change my situation.
I now know that placing the blame on others
keeps me stuck in my past experiences.
I take back the power of responsibility and use this
opportunity to respond and make a change.
Father, teach me to love myself.
From this day forth, I make the decisions that are right for me.
It is well with my soul.
I let go and release it all to you.
In Jesus's name I pray.
Amen

Learn the Lesson

The second thing you will need to do is learn the lesson. Figure out what you need to learn from these experiences and what you are to do with the knowledge. Experiences reflect our inner beliefs. We need to find out what we contributed to this experience. Is there something within me that feels I deserve this experience, and if so, what is it? Having knowledge makes you smart, but knowing how to apply that knowledge is wisdom. Examine these experiences to see how they are all connected. What did you learn from this experience that you can share with others along the way? What are some of the pitfalls that caused you to stumble? What information can you give to the next person to prevent him or her from falling into similar potholes?

How are you going to strengthen others with the lessons you have learned? How do you give them the support they need to go through some of those same life experiences you triumphed? If you do not remember anything else from this book, remember this: out of your tragedy comes life for someone else. I am convinced that we will not be judged on whether or not we love God, but how we treat each other.

Learn to accept and love all aspects of who you are, even your mistakes. Release all your grief, sadness, and loss by writing them down as affirmations. Repeat this process as often as necessary, in order to remove any negative energy from your space and replace it with positive energy.

Sometimes it may seem that we have failed at certain things in our lives. But maybe your succeeding at that moment would have been premature. Maybe you did not learn the information needed to proceed to your next chapter, or perhaps you only received a portion of the information needed. At that point, you did not fail; you just needed the additional time to allow the information to move to the next chapter of your life to catch up with you.

Remember, everything comes to you at the precise moment it has been predetermined to come to you, not a minute or a second sooner. All the information you need to journey on will come to you in its perfect timing, so never stop preparing for it.

PRAYER

Father,
I come to you repenting of all sins, whether knowing
or unknowing, and ask your forgiveness.
I thank you for allowing me the opportunity to gain
knowledge and wisdom from this experience with (you
may insert name of the person, place, or thing).
I thank you that time and chance happen to us all.
Knowing that at the precise time and space, my purpose
(why) will meet with my destiny (what), and I will be
able to use these experiences to strengthen others.
Father, I thank you for allowing me to be the light
that sits on a hill that cannot be hidden.
It is well with my soul.
I let go and release it all to you.
In Jesus's name I pray.
Amen.

Acknowledgment

The third thing you need to do is acknowledge what has happened to you, realizing that life experience was necessary and all part of a bigger plan. God allowed these occurrences in your life to get you to His *expected end*. What does it mean to have an expected end? It means that no matter what situations you face, you are going to accomplish what you were put on this earth to accomplish. It means you will be victorious. No matter what decisions you make in life (right or wrong, good or bad), it will all work together for your good. It all will bring you to the place you were predestined to be.

Start today, and acknowledge the fact that where you are at this very moment is exactly where *I* am supposed to be, in order to do what *I* was created to do. I am on time and in line to reach my destiny. My purpose is much greater than me.

I am reminded of the day I was sitting in my room, meditating. A thought came to me concerning life and the choices we make as individuals. As I thought about all the bad choices I had made, I received the revelation that whatever decision I make (whether good or bad) has already been calculated and accounted for. I was then instructed to do the following exercise.

EXERCISE

Take three steps forward (in any direction) and turn left. Walk three more steps forward and turn left again. Continue and walk three more steps forward and turn left. Walk another three steps and turn left. After I completed this exercise, I noticed that I was headed in the same direction I was in when I first began the exercise. Each left turn represented a wrong decision I made in life, but the end result was that I ended up headed in the same direction I was supposed to be. I was back on track. I do not care how far off track we become; God always has a way of getting us back on track. Remember, nothing can befall on us except it be part of a much bigger plan.

PRAYER

Father,
I come to you repenting of all sins, whether knowing
or unknowing, and ask your forgiveness.
I thank you for allowing me to acknowledge my faults and weaknesses.
I thank you for allowing me to acknowledging that (name
the experience) has happened to me and now it is over.
I thank you that the experience is now in my past and no
longer appearing in the rearview mirror of my future.
I thank you that when I do not approve of the methods
you use to teach me the lessons, I do understand they are
necessary for my growth, destiny, and purpose.
I thank you for reminding me that I can make all the plans I want
pertaining to my life, but it is you who determines my steps.
I thank you my steps are ordered by you.
Father, I release anyone who has ever caused me harm.
I take back my authority and power through
forgiveness of myself and them.
It is well with my soul.
I let go and release it all to you.
In Jesus's name I pray.
Amen

Forgive Others

As I stated, we do not have the capacity to forgive others until we forgive ourselves. You cannot say you forgive someone and continue to carry around the weight or guilt of what has been done to you. Forgiving others does not mean you have to be friends with them or even associate with them. It does mean you are releasing all the hurt, pain, anger, shame, rejection, and negative energy that came from your experience with them. It also means that you have come to the conclusion that what you went through was necessary for your growth. The information you received from that experience will one day be utilized as you walk into your purpose.

People tend to want to forget what they have done to you, said about you, or whatever the case may be. They will come around you as if nothing has ever happened, and that is okay. You can forgive people without them even asking you for your forgiveness. What people give out is a reflection of what is inside of them. If they have not learned to love themselves, they will not be able to love you or anyone else. This is why people run from one relationship to another. They are searching for something in someone else that they do not possess in themselves. Sadly, they have no clue what it is they are searching for.

It is hard to love individuals who, in themselves, do not know what they are searching for. They go from one person to the next, in search of "a thing." After so long in that relationship, they get bored and restless and venture out again. This process will continue until the day they realize the issue lies within them. When they look back and count up the costs, they realize they are indeed broken individuals who have left a trail of other broken people in their past.

When thinking about the very act of forgiveness, I always revert back to the life of Joseph and what transpired when his father died. His brothers remembered all they had done to him. Joseph's brothers first thought was *Now that Father has died, surely Joseph will want to take revenge against us for all that we have done to him.* But Joseph knew, had it not been for these very same acts, he would not have been able to fulfill the promise God gave him as a young boy. Because Joseph was mature in his walk with God, his reply to his brothers was profound: "And Joseph said unto them, Fear not: for am I in the place of God? But as for you, ye thought evil against me; but God meant it unto me for good, to bring to pass, as it is this day, to save much people" (Genesis 50:19, 20 KJV).

They may say you are dwelling on the past, but the reality of the situation is that you have learned the lesson they had to teach you and moved on to the next class. Often, the people responsible for the experiences you gather along life's journey do not realize that they were used as part of a lesson you needed to complete your assignment in the earth realm. You need to ask them the question, "Am I not in the place of God?" Remember that whenever God gives you a promise, He must create a situation conducive to the fulfillment of that promise.

Think about it like this: In school you are given a test. If you fail the test, you must take the test again or repeat the same grade. However, if you pass the test, there is no reason for you take the test again, so you are promoted to the next level.

Exercise

In your mind, get a mental picture of the person who hurt you.

Picture all the feelings you associate with what the person did to you or how it made you feel.

Begin to feel all the emotions you feel or felt.

Begin to gradually release the emotions and feelings associated with this experience until your vision of the person begins to disappear in your mind.

Notice that as you release these emotions and feelings, you begin to feel much lighter.

Begin to affirm the following:

I am thankful for this experience with (you may insert the person, place or thing).

I am thankful for the ability, courage, and strength to forgive (you may insert the person, place or thing).

I forgive you (you may insert the person, place or thing) and wish (you may insert the person, place or thing) well.

PRAYER

Father,
I come to you repenting of all sins, whether knowing
or unknowing, and ask your forgiveness.
I thank you for allowing me to have this experience
with (you may insert the person, place or thing).
I thank you for allowing me to be free from any
and all the negativity of this experience.
I thank you that the experience is now in my past and no
longer appearing in the rearview mirror of my future.
I thank you that by releasing (you may insert the person, place
or thing) I am neither approving their actions nor mine, but
release them with the understanding to know they were making
the best decision they could, given the limited information,
knowledge and understanding they possessed at the time.
I thank you that you have given me the strength to
release (you may insert the person, place or thing).
I thank you that you have given me the ability to set
(you may insert the person, place, or thing) free.
I thank you that I am free.
Father, I release the negative energy and I welcome the positive energy.
It is well with my soul.
I let go and release it all to you.
In Jesus's name I pray.
Amen

Asking for Forgiveness

We are a nation of proud individuals. It is our pride that will not allow us to be vulnerable. Asking someone to forgive us is a hard thing for most of us to do. Because to do so, we are admitting that we have done something wrong. For most of us, our request for forgiveness is generic. We say things like, "If I did anything to you, I ask that you forgive me" or "I apologize if you think I did something wrong to you," or they may just come around and act as though nothing was ever done.

When asking for forgiveness, we need to call out what we have done. We must learn that, as in prayer, when we ask for forgiveness, we must be specific. We must confess what we have done to that person, repent for that wrong, and then ask for their forgiveness. This is an act of confession and repentance. It is only through repentance that we receive forgiveness. Not until then are we completely exonerated by God and the individual we have wronged.

Denying that you have wronged an individual is the worst thing you can do. I was once told that whether you are right or wrong, you cannot tell another person how to feel—and they were right. So, whether or not you did wrong that person, if you are asked to apologize, it is best to do so. Remember, what may not offend you may be offensive to the next person.

It costs us nothing to ask for forgiveness. We need to be

accountable for what we do and what we say to each other. A simple intentional or unintentional action done to someone that caused them pain or an unkind word spoken to or against an individual can be the deciding factor in whether or not that person lives to see another day. We never know what others are going through or just how close to the edge they are living. We all can make sure we treat others the way we want others to treat us.

How we feel about ourselves is exactly what we give to others. The ability to love is the greatest of all the gifts we have been given and can give to others. Love is our birth rite. Every person born was born out of love—the love God has for each of us. There is no such thing as "unplanned" in God's plans. God had already predestined that you would be born on the particular day you were born. God had already written your life's strategy that would bring you to your expected end.

In asking for forgiveness, our egos may take a blow, but we will radiate love, the love of God that lives within us that we want to share with others. If we do not ask for forgiveness when we wrong others, how can we expect others to ask our forgiveness when they wrong us? How can we expect God to forgive us when we have yet to forgive the person who has wronged us?

PRAYER

Father,
I come to you repenting of all sins, whether knowing
or unknowing, and ask your forgiveness.
I thank you that you are quick to rebuke me when I am wrong.
I thank you that you cause my spirit to be convicted
when I stand in judgment of others.
I thank you for the humility to confess, repent, and ask
forgiveness from those whom I have wronged.
I thank you that this experience is greater than
myself or the person I have wronged.
I thank you that it costs nothing to love for it is my birthright.
Father, I release all the negativity and ask that you
reconcile any relationships that have been severed due
to this experience that I will need in the future.
It is well with my soul.
I let go and release it all to you.
In Jesus's name I pray.
Amen

Be Thankful

I hear you saying, *Why do I need to be thankful?* They have done nothing for me except bring me a lot of heartache and pain. Being thankful means you have matured from where you were when that experience took place. You have now realized that what has occurred in your life is part of a much bigger picture, one that will bring you to your expected end. The *win*. It was what you went through in your experiences with those people that has allowed you to see what lies inside of you. These life experiences are the basis for your stance in life. These experiences will soon become the foundation on which you are to build.

Thank them for the experiences you shared. Thank them for the knowledge you gained from the experience. Then thank them because now you have the strength to forgive them. Remember, forgiving people is not merely saying the words "I forgive you" and walking away. Forgiveness is saying the words "I forgive you" and walking away with the assurance that your experience with that person or event was necessary for your now, the person you are at this moment.

Be thankful that God has chosen you to go through these experiences because He knew you could handle it. He knew you would be victorious. Remember, you are at your expected end. Where you are at this precise moment is where you were predestined to be before you were formed in your mother's womb.

Before the foundation of the world, before you were even thought of, God knew there would someday be a you, who would do what you did, live where you live, work were you work, encounter the people you have encountered, and live the experiences you have lived.

God also knew that one day, it would take all those experiences you have had to reach the people assigned to you and those you are assigned to reach. I promise you that not one drop of your life's experiences has been unwarranted, and nothing you have encountered will be lost. Everything will work for your good. It has already worked on your behalf.

PRAYER

Father,
I come to you repenting of all sins, whether knowing
or unknowing, and ask your forgiveness.
I thank you for the opportunity you have given me to go
through the experiences set before me, knowing that each
obstacle faced brought me closer to my expected end.
I am thankful that you have blessed me and my
life to be a vessel to carry others to safety.
Father, it is my prayer that all will soon see how great
you are and that your plans for our lives are bigger
than we can imagine, dream, or even think.
I release all doubt and negativity associated with these experiences.
It is well with my soul.
I let go and release it all to you.
In Jesus's name I pray.
Amen

Painful Purpose

By now, you are wondering what your purpose can possibly be. God already knew what and who you were to become before you were formed in your mother's womb. He knew the exact amount of trials that you would need to face and exactly what it would take to get you to your purpose to fulfill your destiny. He also knew the exact date and time and even the place that you would overcome those trials.

The road to your purpose may have been painful but necessary. You have experienced love and loss, success and failure. You have been faced with moments of inspiration and creativity, as well as struggles and doubt. Whether good or bad, you have to make the decision to walk through the fire.

This road is not about what others want you to be or even what you yourself want to be. This road is about you becoming what and who you were created to become and what you were created to do.

No matter what situation life throws at you, remember, you were created to *win*. Your life was predestined to be successful. All things will work together for your good. Nothing that you do takes God by surprise. He has already written our lives; all our failures, successes, misjudgments, ups and downs.

God's Will is the ultimate governing factor. Each of our wills is centered inside of His. There are no wrong decisions, only opportunities for learning and growing. Although God's will is perfect for our lives and He has allowed us free will inside His will, he has already allotted time for our decisions and failures. At the precise moment when time and chance meet, we will find ourselves fulfilling our purpose and walking in our destiny.

Remember, as you journey through life, your purpose is being revealed over time, little by little with each experience and lesson learned. Like peeling an onion, part of your purpose has already been revealed. Maybe it is not visible to the naked eye, but it will soon manifest. It is the experiences in your past that prepare and equip you for your future.

Do not take any experience or person you meet for granted or ignore the details of those experiences. It is in the details where the clues to your purpose lie. Remember, everything happens for a reason. Often, the thing that gives us so much adversity is the very thing in which our purpose lies. These are experiences that may not seem to have a solution or end. We all have been equipped to help others, to make the world a better place. We may not even see how we will overcome the situation or why we had to go through it. But once we learn how to overcome it, we are able to share with others to aid them in overcoming their issues.

Life is a process that prepares you to live the purpose for which you were created. It is a process designed to take you through experience (whether good or bad) after experience, to help you become all you are destined to become. We are constantly learning and growing. As long as we remain on earth, we will learn consciously and subconsciously. When we stop learning, we cease to exist in this world.

Learning is the process of *perfecting* who we are over a period of time; realizing new things or things we were too busy to notice before; learning how to look at life experiences from a higher perspective; learning to look at them through love, grace, and with a positive attitude; knowing that in the end we all will *win*.

PRAYER

Father,
I come to you repenting of all sins, whether knowing
or unknowing, and ask your forgiveness.
I thank you for the purpose you have set before me.
I thank you that although it was painful, you
have brought me to my expected end.
I thank you for the growth in loving and caring for others.
I thank you for teaching me the forgiveness of myself and others.
I thank you for showing me that love for you, myself,
and others is the greatest gift anyone can give.
Father, I denounce any negative energy I may
have created throughout my transitions.
I ask that those whom I have wronged forgive me
as I forgive those who have wronged me.
I thank you for the strength to forgive and ask for forgiveness.
It is well with my soul.
I let go and release it all to you.
In Jesus's name I pray.
Amen

Beauty for Ashes

What does it mean to be victorious? It means you have successfully overcome your struggles against all odds. Being victorious is more than winning. It is more than being an overcomer. Being victorious is about living through something that was meant to destroy you and deter you from reaching your destiny. It is being able to walk away from the situation with a sense that you will use those life experiences to help those you are assigned to help.

Being victorious means you have learned to love yourself in spite of all you have gone through. You have learned to love every aspect of your entire being, even your unlovable attributes. You have learned not to overlook your faults but to effect change to become the best person you can be for you and the world at large.

Remember, people can only control you for as long as you allow them to. Refuse to continue to be the victim. Take back your power. Stop blaming others for how your life has turned out or for you not accomplishing all you set out to accomplish. Accept the responsibility as being yours and yours alone. Vow to change it by making the decisions that are right for you. Again, there are no wrong decisions, only learning opportunities.

Love yourself enough to release the people and things attached to you that no longer serve purpose in your life. As stated earlier, all of creation has a purpose it *must* fulfill. Sometimes when creation is used for something other than its intended purpose, it becomes perverted. Do not allow anyone or anything to pervert you or your purpose. You were created to *win*.

PRAYER

Father,
I come to you repenting of all sins, whether knowing
or unknowing, and ask your forgiveness.
I thank you for allowing me the opportunity to
experience these life-changing moments.
I thank you for giving me beauty for ashes. The ashes of decisions
that I deemed as wrong, judgments, unforgiveness, lack of love,
and all the negative energy I spewed out into the universe.
I now know that it is you who holds my future and not I myself.
I thank you for the strength and courage to exact change in my life
that is not a reflection of your heart, whether for myself or others.
I thank you that you have shown me my purpose,
my strengths, and my weaknesses.
I thank you that at the precise moment when time and chance shall
meet, you will make sure I am ready to walk into my destiny.
Father, it is well with my soul.
I let go and release it all to you.
In Jesus's name I pray.
Amen

Note: Strive to plant the best seeds possible. There is a law of sowing and reaping. Always remember that the harvest is *always* bigger than the seed planted.

References

Adams, Yolanda, "More than a Melody," *More Than a Melody*, Tribute Records, 1995, track 6.

Houston, Whitney, "Greatest Love of All," *Whitney Houston*, Arista Records, 1985, track 9.

Printed in the United States
By Bookmasters